Maverick

I Dream of being a Nokota

Karen Swasey

Edited by Lil Barcaski

Published by: GWN Publishing
www.GWNPublishing.com

Cover Design: Kristina Conatser

Paperback ISBN: 978-1-965971-29-1

Dedication

This book is dedicated to RiverView Farm and their unwavering commitment to rescue horses—

a place where hope, healing, and new beginnings are made possible.

To every soul that has devoted their time and heart to giving these magnificent creatures a second chance,

your compassion inspires us to honor life and our roots.

Find and order my other books by visiting my website: myseaofgrace.com

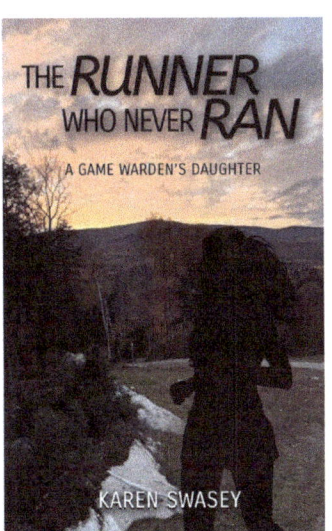

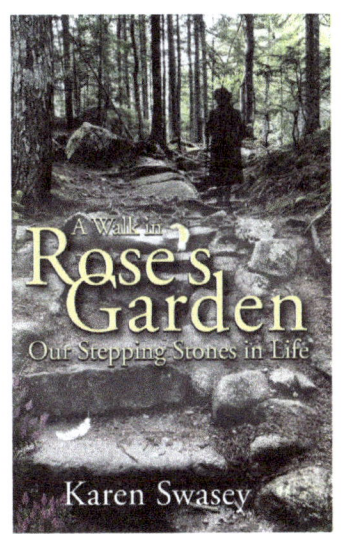

Contents

"The Nokota horse represents the spirit of freedom and the resilience of the plains, a living legacy of strength and beauty."
—Unknown

Prologue

T his is a story of hope and resilience, highlighting the connection to heritage and the journey of exploring possibilities and dreams. Maverick dreams of running free in the Little Missouri Badlands of North Dakota as a Nokota horse, known as the last of the wild horse population in this region. As a rescue horse, Maverick embraces the spirit of the Nokota horse, imagining feathers in his mane as symbolic ties to his heritage, enhancing the enchantment of his story. Readers and enthusiasts alike will find inspiration in the breed's resilience and heritage, crafting narratives that celebrate their legacy. The story will share the gift of what a rescue horse can bring to those who receive the gift of the heart of a horse—a true guardian and steadfast companion, resonating with themes of trust and mutual respect.

I Dream of Being a Nokota!

Hello, my name is Maverick. I am a pony that lives in Maine at a rescue farm in Lisbon Falls called RiverView Farm. We have about 46 horses of all shapes and sizes living here on the farm, along with a couple of donkeys and a sheep named Eddie.

I was rescued when I was very little, so little that I didn't even have my teeth yet! I was a baby foal when someone found me. I was really scared and didn't know what to do, but I had heard the other horses talking about people coming to look at us, so I was hoping someone would take me home. There were three other "ponies" there with me who needed homes as well. We were really needing care and I wasn't sure what was going to happen to us, so I could hardly wait for the day that people came to look at us.

Then the day came... there was this beautiful lady who showed up like an angel. She looked at me and said, "No worries my little friend, I will take care of you." She unloaded me and my three other pony friends off the horse trailer. The people who delivered me exclaimed that an old man up north couldn't take care of us anymore. That's funny, I thought; my friend CeeCee has an auction number on her, meaning she was supposed to be for sale, but my new angel just smiled and said, "I'll take them all."

Just to give you a clue of my physical state, when we arrived at my new home, I was a little bit of a mess. You see, my prior owner didn't take very good care of me, and I didn't know how much until I met my angel friend. My hair was all matted, I had lice and I was malnourished. This meant that I was really hungry, so I went around trying to find a mare where I could nurse. Unfortunately, the people who had me when I was born, took me from my mother before I was weened, and I didn't know how to eat anything but milk.

I searched for a mare who might let me get close enough to drink milk. I found a mare, but she wasn't impressed and she let me have it. The fact was, she wasn't able to help me anyway. My new angel friend was watching me closely. It was then that this angel who rescued me realized that I was a baby foal and not just another pony that she was told she was rescuing. We were all such a mess, she couldn't see that I was actually a baby. She gave me a bath to clean me up from all the dirt they left on me and then she brushed me and cleaned my hoofs. I didn't have any teeth yet, so she had to feed me too! What a gift it was to have someone who cared about me! My other friends and I were so thankful that we had someone who gave us the extra care we needed; she truly was an angel delivered to us.

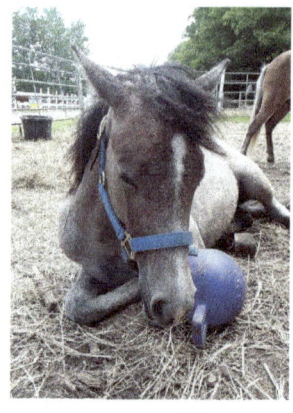

As time went on, and I was growing up, I would have visitors stop by and I would meet all kinds of people who had their horses boarded at the farm.

I then learned that a rescue farm does these sorts of things frequently. They rescue horses that are no longer wanted or that people can no longer care for. It is essential to have these kinds of angels, as there are many others like me who are in need.

Finally, I was safe and clean with a full belly ready to play with my friends. But wait, something new was about to happen!

A few months went by and I was strong and frisky and playing in the paddock with the other horses and my friends. The people at the farm would take me on walks with them, and I became the cute little baby foal that everyone wanted to see.

As I grew older, the time came that I needed to be put up for adoption. This was to find my forever person who would love me and support my care. There is something I also need to share with you, when the angel who rescued me puts up her horses for adoption, she looks for someone who would like to keep them here at the farm. Oh, my goodness! I was so excited to learn this!! So, I waited to see who this person was going to be.

One day, this man and woman showed up to take a peek at me and to give me snuggles. They were really kind. I made sure I was on my best behavior as I crawled into their heart. I batted my soft eyes and I let the woman snuggle my neck. I knew from the moment she saw me that I was going to be hers. The man was large in stature, but he was truly a gentle giant. He would take me for walks and help my new mama brush me. Most importantly, he provided the brute strength needed to clean out the paddock and always made sure I had fresh shavings to sleep in at night.

My life from that day forward created a bond that I didn't even know could exist. I would watch to see when my mom and dad would drive into the yard and I would run to the fence so that I could greet them and snuggle them with my warm, soft nose. I could tell they loved me with all their heart, and I just knew, I would never be alone again.

Everyone was very curious about my color as I was very unique and they would try and guess what my breed might be. But there was something inside of me that told me I was different, and that I had a heritage that was as unique as my color. I would have these dreams of my ancestors roaming through beautiful mountains and valleys in what is called the Dakota's, or the badlands of North Dakota.

The horses in my dreams had feathers in their manes and they were painted with colorful symbols on their bodies.

I would see them running free across the hills and mountains where they came down from Canada. I also had dreams of my ancestors who were roaming the hills of Ireland and England. In my dreams, I saw these beautiful lush green rolling hills and I wondered about the history behind the scenes. These dreams returned again and again like it was showing me a story that I held inside.

And then one day, someone showed up at the barn and walked over to the fence and said, "Is this horse a Nokota Horse?" He looked so perplexed as he stared at me with his mouth wide open. My friend Kari, (a beautiful palomino mare), was being visited by her mom and she had brought her friend, this man, to the barn to visit Kari.

Kari's mom came over to the fence to hear what he was saying. Her friend just stood there looking at me and said, "Did you know that this horse has the form and color of a Nokota horse?" The man was from the Midwest and knew of the breed and their history. I came closer to listen to what he was saying. *Oh my, could this be those dreams I have had since I was a little foal, of my ancestors being wild and running free?*

The man continued sharing the story of the Nokota horse and how the horse's history goes back to the Great Plains of the Midwest and that they were an integral part of the lives of the Nakota people. He shared that the Nokota horse was more than just an animal; it was a lifeline for the Nakota tribe. He went on and shared the story of how this breed carried the Nakota tribe through battles, hunts, and migrations, embodying the spirit of resilience that defines the heart of the Nakota people.

He said, "These horses have a strong sense of loyalty and intelligence, which allows them to form close bonds with their riders, becoming an essential part of the Nakota community."

I stood there blinking my soft eyes excited to hear more of what I believed must be the story of my ancestors, or so my dreams revealed.

When my mom came to the barn, Kari's mom was excited to share the story of her friend who was mesmerized by my appearance and how he was convinced I was a Nokota horse. This sparked an interest in my heritage at the farm, so my mom and the angel who rescued me became intrigued and began to learn more about the story behind the Nokota horse.

I stood there listening and thinking, little did they know that I had been dreaming of these tales since I was a little foal. And so, the research began, going through the chapters of time about the Nokota horse. My story goes like this....

The Dream of My Ancestors

Sometimes, when I dream of my ancestors, I imagine them roaming freely over the vast northern plains of the Midwest. On other nights, my dreams take me to the rolling hills of Europe. In listening to my mom, I discovered that the Nokota horse breed was once almost extinct—a rare breed of wild horses known to roam the rugged Little Missouri Badlands of North Dakota. It was like my dreams were coming to life!

The other remarkable aspect I learned is that this breed of horse is known to be associated with the Native American leader Sitting Bull, a Hunkpapa Lakota who was regarded as a holy man. It is believed that these feral horses are descendants of local  Native American ponies, which were a mix of Thoroughbreds, Colonial Spanish horses, draft and harness breeds from the 19th century, dating from 1801 to 1900.

"We learned that my bloodlines were a blend of Fell Pony, Belgian Draft, and the Tukoman Horse, each contributing qualities such as strength, endurance, and elegance, which adds depth to this dream and aligns with the character of the Nokota horse. This along with my blue roan coloring added a distinct and striking appearance, echoing the idea of a unique resemblance to the Nokota breed. You can find out more here; https://vetmed.tamu.edu/animalgenetics/horse-ancestry/

It is considered possible that the Nakota people may have had horses resembling the Nokota breed among their herds. While much of the connection between Sitting Bull's horses and the foundation of the Nokota breed, it relies mostly on their local legend and oral history rather than documented evidence. The breed itself is believed to have developed from a blend of ranch horses, Native American horses, and Spanish Mustangs native to the Northern Plains. Some accounts suggest that horses connected to the Lakota and Nakota peoples could have contributed to the genetic makeup of the Nokota horse, although the overall origins of the breed are more broadly tied to the regional horse populations than to any single lineage or event.

The story continues like this; It is thought that in the early to mid-1700s, some of the wild descendants of these colonial horses migrated across the Great Northern Plains, known today as the Dakotas. Historical accounts indicate that a branch of the Sioux who lived in the woodlands of Eastern Minnesota—the Lakota tribe—were displaced by the Chippewa and subsequently became new inhabitants of the expansive northern plains. Both the Lakota and Nakota people trace their roots to the ancient tribes of these Eastern Woodlands.

Over time, migration and adaptation to different environments led to the emergence of distinct groups within the Great Sioux Nation. This Great Sioux Nation, also known as the Oceti Sakowin, is divided into three major groups: the Dakota, Nakota, and Lakota. The differentiation among these groups is a testament to their resilience and ability to adapt to changing landscapes and circumstances, which also influenced the development of horse breeds associated with them. These groups represent distinct dialects and cultural practices but they share a common lineage that dates back centuries. The Lakota people primarily inhabit the Northern Plains, while the Nakota people reside in regions that include parts of North and South Dakota including Montana. Despite these divisions, their ancestral connection remains a fundamental aspect of their identity. Imagine their delight and amazement when encountering these magnificent horses! This meeting of these feral horses would impact each of their destinies and change their lives forevermore.

Reflecting upon the heritage and legacy of the Great Sioux Nation, I am profoundly moved by the unwavering spirit that defines the Nakota, Lakota, and Dakota peoples. Through generations of challenge, migration, and adaptation, their resilience has shone like a beacon—illuminating a path of strength, honor, and dignity.

The Great Sioux Nation stands as a living testament to perseverance. The Nakota, Lakota, and Dakota are not only keepers of the land, but also guardians of tradition, memory, and wisdom. Their steadfast commitment to their heritage and to each other is a reminder of the power of unity and the enduring value of cultural roots.

In honoring the Sioux Nation, we recognize a legacy that stretches beyond time—a legacy built upon courage, respect for the earth, and an unbreakable bond between people and the land they call home. May we continue to honor and learn from this spirit, striving ourselves to walk with humility and reverence for all that has been entrusted to us by those who came before us.

My mom did some research in the Cowgirl Magazine by Deborah Donahue and it said, *"The Nomadic Lakota had, up until this time, been dependent upon dogs to pull their travois (a type of sled consisting of two joined poles). Domesticating the newly discovered "wild species" who the Lakota called "Sunka Wakans" or "Sacred Dogs" would not only alter the Lakota's means of transport, of both people and goods, but would, in time, serve to make them expert horsemen—and breeders of horses that would prove superior both on the hunt and on the battlefield. The Lakota became the first light cavalry in the world, whose influence and power extended across the Northern Plain."*

Imagine their excitement to now have this amazing horse to help them hunt and travel across the Dakotas.

She learned that in the 1800's, when Theodore Roosevelt was ranching in the Little Missouri Badlands of North Dakota, these horses had been confiscated from the Lakota's, the breed known as the Nokota® breed. This was done to limit the Lakota's mobility and ensure the tribe's compliance after the U.S. Calvary loss at the battle of "Little Big Horn." At that time the horse itself was thought to be of little value and was less desirable to the local ranchers as they thought them to be poor saddle stock, too small, too scruffy, and too colorful, like being a blue roan like me! Little did they realize their importance, but one man took notice.

Then the horses were discovered by a Frenchman named Marquis De Mores, who saw beyond their outward appearance and recognized their remarkable endurance, intelligence, and compact build. He purchased 250 of them, drawn by their unique qualities. The Marquis, a visionary entrepreneur, was captivated by the Nokota horses' ability to thrive in harsh conditions and their unyielding spirit. He believed these traits made them ideal for a variety of tasks, from ranch work to endurance riding. His investment marked the beginning of the Nokota horses' transformation—from being overlooked to becoming celebrated symbols of resilience and adaptability. His decision to invest in the Nokota horses marked the beginning of their journey from being undervalued to being celebrated.

Marquis De Mores' acquisition of the horses not only preserved their lineage, but also sparked interest in their unique characteristics. Under his care, the Nokota horses flourished, showcasing their resilience and versatility to a broader audience. His efforts in promoting the Nokota horses set a precedent for others, encouraging the recognition of their cultural and historical significance.

And so it was, these true Native American ponies reflected their robust nature with their feathered ankles and thick, manes and tails. Their striking appearance was matched by their extraordinary endurance and intelligence, qualities that endeared them to the Lakota people. The Lakota were particularly renowned for their blue roan war horses. This rare yet dominant color in the Nokota population was not only a mark of beauty but also a symbol of strength and resilience.

The Lakota people revered these horses, seeing in them the embodiment of their own spirit and tenacity. No wonder the friend of Kari's mom was so stunned. I am a blue roan and this description is exactly like me!

Fell Pony Horse Breed Profile

They have been all but forgotten, these Canadian horses, even though they were widely admired as late as the Civil War. They likely influenced generations of Indian ranch and farming horses in the Dakotas, and their feral brethren are well known. From what my dreams have revealed, it is just like the Fell Pony breed from Europe. These horses look just like me!!

In 1884 De Mores sold 60 of these Sioux mares to AC Huidekoper. Huidekoper was a breeder of Percheron's, a draft horse known for their intelligence and willingness to work. They were enormously popular as an all-around farming and driving horse. He wanted to create a superior line of ranch horses and felt that Indian horses were a good foundation stock for crossbreeding. So, he bred his Sioux mares to the Percheron stallions, which were called the "American horses." These true Indian ponies reflected their robust nature with feathered ankles and thick mains and tails.

"So, here is my bloodline again all entwined with the story of the Nokota horse. Could it be that this nice man from the Midwest was an angel himself bringing me the gift of bringing my dreams to a reality?!!"

Oh, but this next revelation is truly the lasting gift that was bestowed upon the breed of the Nokota horse, meet a miracle in history!

An Unexpected Surprise

H ere is the story I learned of a famous person in history, and his connection with my ancestors. In American history, it is said that few figures stand as tall and enduring as Theodore Roosevelt, the 26th President of the United States. Known for his robust charisma and adventurous spirit, Roosevelt's life was a tapestry woven with threads of many diverse experiences. Among these threads was his profound admiration for the Nakota people and their mastery of equestrian skills. He was amazed by their ability to navigate the rugged terrain with ease. In his writings, he described the Nakota riders as "centaurs," seamlessly merging human and horse into a single, fluid entity and grace. This reverence was not merely a passing fancy; it was a deep respect for a culture that harmonized with nature and valued the bond between human and animal. The Nokota horse, revered by the Nakota people, was more than a means of transportation. It was a symbol of their spiritual connection to the land and a crucial part of their ceremonial life. Roosevelt marveled at the Nakota's ability to communicate with their horses through subtle gestures and an almost telepathic understanding. His encounters with the Nokota horse and its riders left an indelible mark on his legacy. He often reflected on the lessons he learned from the Nakota people—lessons of resilience, respect for nature, and the importance of preserving cultural heritage. These experiences shaped his policies and his outlook on conservation, leaving a lasting impact on American history, and little did he realize what gift was about to happen to protect this amazing breed of horse.

Theodore Roosevelt National Park was established in 1947. Its primary aim was to protect the breathtaking badlands and the native species that thrived within them. But little did anyone know that the park's lands were home to a remarkable treasure: the Nokota horses. These horses, revered by the Nakota people for their endurance, agility, and spiritual significance, had roamed the plains for generations. It wasn't until the late 20th century that the presence of Nokota horses in the park came to light. Researchers and park rangers, while conducting wildlife surveys, stumbled upon a herd of horses exhibiting distinct characteristics and behaviors. Their endurance, agility, and unique bond with the land were unmistakable. Further investigation revealed that these were indeed the Nokota horse, descendants of those that had been integral to the Nakota people's way of life.

This discovery of Nokota horses in Theodore Roosevelt National Park sparked a wave of excitement and reverence. Recognizing their historical and cultural significance, park authorities and conservationists quickly moved to ensure their protection. The laws governing the national park, originally intended to preserve the natural landscapes and native wildlife, were now extended to safeguard these magnificent horses, the Nokota horse.

And there it is... the story to how my breed was protected evermore through a sanctuary that I believe was a prayer from the Nakota people, that these horses would be protected and that their story, and the story of my ancestors are kept alive.

RiverView Farm: A Place Where Dreams Come True

Here's the story I've learned about RiverView Farm. The angel who rescued me as a baby is a person of unwavering perseverance and determination, reminiscent of Nokota's spirit. Her grandfather owned some land, and, driven by her love of horses and memories of time spent at her grandmother's farm, she was determined, by the age of 17, to purchase some of this land and start her own horse farm. With her grandmother's support as a co-signer, she worked incredibly hard and made her dream a reality.

If you look at the farm today, it's hard to imagine it was once nothing but dense woods. The open fields, now enjoyed by the horses, were painstakingly cleared piece by piece. By 2000, she cared for 12 horses, and around 2006, she built an indoor arena on the property—a metal structure with stalls along the sides and a combined living area and tack room.

Then, in February 2009, a fierce storm known as the "Super Bowl storm" swept through, covering the area with ice and snow. While everyone was gathered at a friend's house watching the game, (after caring for the horses), someone rushed in and told her she needed to go to the barn immediately. At first glance, the barn's front seemed untouched, but when she opened the door, she saw that the arena had collapsed at the back due to the weight of the snow and ice. Miraculously, the horses in the stalls along the edges were unharmed and were even stomping for their dinner, a testament to the protection provided by her perseverance—and perhaps the land itself.

Despite the setback, she remained determined, removed the damaged building, and learned that five similar barns had suffered the same fate due to roofing problems. Refusing to give up, she pressed forward with her dream of RiverView Farm.

Between 2012 and 2015, another powerful storm struck. This one arrived unexpectedly in the middle of the night—a sudden microburst swept through, tearing the entire roof off the barn. Remarkably, everyone, including the horses inside at the time, escaped unharmed, and it was only later they learned that several other barns in the area had suffered significant damage. Once again, it seemed as though a protective force watched over them, shielding the farm and its animals from harm. The sense of ancestral protection and her deep love for the horses continued to safeguard RiverView Farm through every challenge.

Her dream to create a rescue farm—a refuge where people and horses alike could heal and feel safe—remained undeterred. Year after year, she expanded the space, welcoming more horses in need. Today, RiverView Farm is home to over 40  horses, some boarded, some rescued, and has become a sanctuary where visitors experience the healing power of the land and the gentle presence of the horses. It all began with the perseverance of a young woman, just 17 years old, who got up with the dawn and worked tirelessly to build a haven for both horses and the human spirit.

 RiverView Farm Inc. is a horse boarding facility located in Lisbon Falls, Maine, offering a comprehensive range of services including boarding, training, and lessons. The farm features two outdoor rings and a round pen for training and exercise, along with miles of scenic trails for riding and exploration. Horses are accommodated in spacious stalls and large shelters, which are cleaned weekly and provided with fresh bedding. Free choice hay is available 24/7, allowing the horses to graze all day as mother nature intended. In addition, grain is offered up to three times daily by experienced staff members who use high-quality feeds to support each horse's nutritional needs.

RiverView Farm also offers horse leasing options, geriatric horse care, horse retirement services, horse training and rehabilitation programs, and riding lessons for all ages and levels—as well as a summer day camp for kids.

RiverView Farm recently hosted a benefit dinner for First Foundation Inc., a nonprofit supporting youth and adults transitioning out of foster care. The farm actively participates in local events and provides outreach to individuals who have experienced trauma, offering a space where they can connect with the healing spirit of the horses and the land.

"My angel's vision is for everyone who visits RiverView Farm to discover a true place of refuge—a sanctuary where safety and the unique, therapeutic healing that only horses provide are always present. She wholeheartedly embraces the rich tradition of the 4-H Club, hoping this tradition continues to flourish throughout Maine for children of all ages. It is a legacy that deserves to live on, offering kids the chance to experience the gift and the rewarding work of caring for a horse. At RiverView Farm, the mission endures: come, connect with the land and the spirit of the horse, and let us continue saving and uplifting lives, one person at a time."

RiverView Farm: My Friend Kari's Story

"Introducing Kari" written by Jo-Jean Keller

Y ou may read about Kari and feel I made a decision that probably wasn't the most advisable! However, Kari gives me a sense of peace and comfort like no other. She's the best gift I've ever given myself!

I spent my younger years in Paducah, Ky riding ponies and creating outdoor adventures with make-believe cowboys and Indians! After moving to Louisville, my pony adventures were no more!

I was otherwise occupied with life for many years and had little horse contact. I had since moved to Maine, and woke up one morning and said to myself, "If I don't start riding again now, when am I going to? Why wait?"

RiverView Farm was right down the road. After one visit, I knew this was where I wanted to start my new horse adventure! I found I could lease a horse and take lessons! Although I was pretty much sure I knew all I needed to know about riding, I was all in! I quickly discovered that when it came to horses and riding, I was less knowledgeable than I realized.

After taking lessons, riding, learning, lunging, and generally reacquainting myself with horses, it was time to think about getting a horse of my own! Rather than visiting local horses, I fell in love with a photo of a horse on Facebook. It brought back childhood memories of loving horses—especially Palominos, my favorites since watching Roy Rogers and his horse, Trigger.

That special horse, "Zippos Carmel Bar," was part of an Appaloosa Breeding Farm that, due to personal reasons, was going out of business and liquidating their stock. Although I had some very good advice from Lisa Bosse to search locally instead, I was determined that Kari was the horse I wanted.

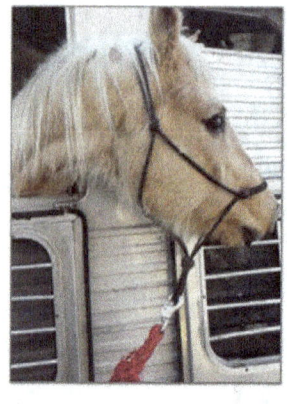 After what seemed like an avalanche of paperwork and endless delays, Kari was due to arrive in January 2014. I was beyond excited. At that time, I was the Children's Librarian in Lisbon, Maine. The library was right on Main St. (the route the transport would travel to the farm) and I stayed by the window the entire morning, with prior permission of course. Finally, a huge horse transport made the turn and headed up Main Street!

I seemingly moved faster than the speed of light (well, almost) and made it to the farm right as the transport made its turn into the RiverView Driveway. I couldn't wait to see Kari step off the ramp. She was beautiful and much larger in reality than I had envisioned. The transport driver said she had traveled well and he'd had several offers to buy her!

My next adventure was officially on its way! Little did I know what an adventure (and challenge) it would be!

Kari had been a broodmare in her earlier life. Although she had six-months of training under saddle with a respected trainer, she was not really accustomed to the attention she would receive in an active stable setting with a variety of horses and people! She was also highly reactive to unusual situations (and they were all unusual to her).

She had had a medical checkup and the necessary shots before leaving Illinois. After her arrival, we had her checked by our vet, including her eyes to make sure there was no physical reason for her reactions.

I was extremely fortunate to have Lisa's wisdom and guidance over the next years. The first couple of years were the most difficult with a couple of unexpected dismounts and a dislocated shoulder. I quickly learned (and have relearned many times) that many problems are caused by the rider's inattention or poor judgment. As I continued to practice breathing and patience, I began to build a lasting relationship with Kari. The better our relationship became, the less reactive and anxious she was.

Along with Lisa, I had several resources that gave me inspiration and direction.

Bless the Clicker and Hay Stretcher!

I had not really paid much attention to the concept of clicker training until I got Kari. Once I understood how easy it was to use, I was hooked!

I found the book "Clicker Training for Your Horse" by Alexandra Kurland, and used it as reference.

As I had mentioned previously, Kari was anxious and reactive around the farm. Shadows, black hoses (the black hose of death found everywhere and waiting to strike), changes in the immediate environment (such as a hay bale in a new spot) all could trigger her reactions.

I introduced Kari to the clicker and the magic hay stretcher in the small round pen. I had a bag full of surprises, such as bubbles, balls, hats, tambourines, handkerchiefs and scarves. I included anything I could think of that might trigger a response.

I left her loose and introduced an item. If she stood quietly and looked, I gave her a click and a reward. We started with a hat. Once she stood, looked it over and got her click and reward, I moved the hat closer to her nose. Again, she stood quietly and earned her reward. The big change came when she touched her nose to the hat and sniffed it, licked it, and generally accepted it into her category of known items that cause no  harm. We moved to putting the hat on her head, which was not a problem once she had accepted it.

The tambourine was accepted fairly quickly in the same way as the hat. The big difference, of course, was when I tapped it. The noise was not necessarily welcome and Kari backed away. For the continuation of this lesson, I walked slowly around the round pen, hoping that Kari's natural curiosity would encourage her to follow and she did. We had a mini parade around the round pen and she earned her clicks and rewards periodically.

The biggest challenge was the bubbles! She was definitely not interested in the small round things floating aimlessly around her. We spent some quality time becoming acquainted with the bubbles and accepting them.

I am currently using the clicker to encourage her to lower her head and keep it lowered. As with the other challenges, this is well-worth the effort and patience needed.

Kari is very attuned to her environment and we take the time to examine anything she notes that is new and different. She approaches, sniffs, and touches whatever she's concerned with and then we walk on. It's great to see how curious she is and how confident she has become with changes around the farm. As we were grooming recently, we were able to observe a front-end loader loading manure into a dump truck. She looked with interest and relaxed again.

One of our biggest successes was training her to accept her spring shots. The first vet visit involved an unhappy Kari in a stall. Once I mentioned to Dr. Bonny that I was clicker training Kari, she told me to pinch her neck, click, and reward her, then add a poke with a toothpick. Once she was comfortable with the pinch, I added the toothpick. Now, shots are considerably easier for all concerned. Dr. Bonny gives her a shot, tells me to click, and Dr. Bonny's assistant gives Kari a reward. Less stress for all!

Clicker training has made a huge difference in our relationship!

Kari's story is written and shared by her mom Jo-Jean Keller.

The Blue Roan...My Uniqueness

The Nokota horse is commonly blue roan in color, which I have, as I am grayish and have a bluish color skin. I have a mixture of black and white hair and my legs have what looks like black stockings. I even have a few red hairs mixed in as well.

I have a beautiful gait, which is an ambling gait like a Nokota. It is called the "Indian shuffle," which means that I have a very soft canter when I run. I am very excited for my mom to enjoy riding me so I can show her how gentle I can be as she has to be very careful as not to hurt herself.

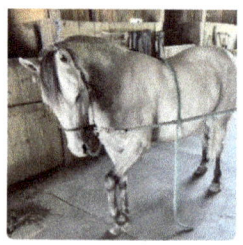

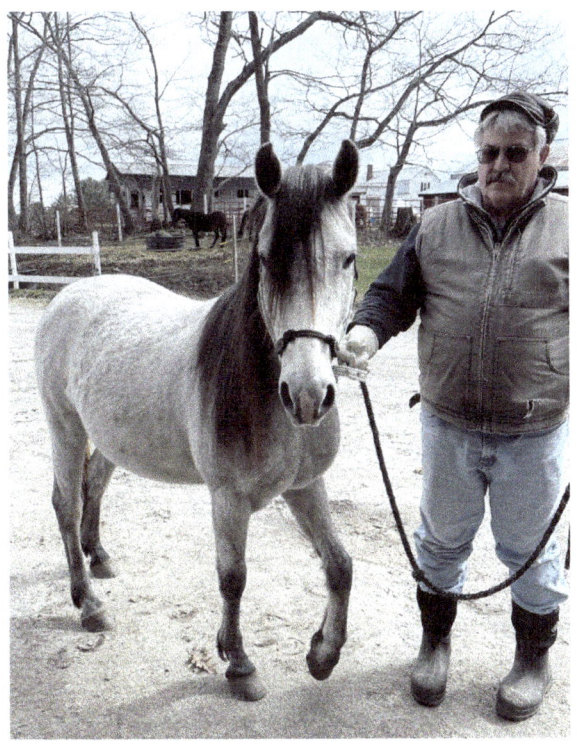

"*I am a descendant of Sitting Bull's war ponies. My ancestors carried his warriors in the fight against Custer at the Battle of the Little Big Horn. On these Northern Plains, my homeland, I have endured now for more than one hundred and fifty snows. Through my veins flows the lifeblood of history, and the stories of great warriors.*"—*Courtesy of NHC, by Deborah Donahue*

"Maverick, my true guardian and steadfast companion, together we resonate the themes of trust and mutual respect. His loyalty and protective nature mirror the dedication and love inherent in the breed's history."

Healing Hoofs: Touched by the Spirit of the Horse

I have learned a very important piece of my heritage; it is the connection that I feel with my human friends. It is known that the Nokota horse history is a theme of renewal, connection, and a journey of finding one's place in the world. The enduring spirit of my ancestors resonates within me, a profound healing that touches the depths of the soul, drawing others to me with an undeniable curiosity. This came to light as truth in this next story...

A lady at the barn where I live shared one afternoon that there was "just something different about me." My presence offers a soft gift of "hope" and "resilience" which is written time and time again as a reference within my legacy as a Nokota horse. She referenced the power of "Equine Therapy" which is a gift like non other.

The "gift" is shared like this... Few experiences in life are as profoundly calming and grounding as standing in the presence of a horse. With their steady gaze, gentle demeanor, and innate ability to sense human emotions, horses possess a healing presence that touches the deepest corners of one's soul. Their quiet majesty invites us to slow down, breathe deeply, and reconnect with the essence of who we are. This unique connection forms the foundation of equine therapy, a transformative practice that offers immense benefits for mental health and overall well-being. This is what happens at our barn each and every day, and as a rescue horse, I want to share a story my mom shared with me about a big beautiful red gelding she rescued years ago.

Many years ago, my mom experienced a profound moment of healing. At the time, she was overwhelmed by stress and anxiety, but this transformative moment brought her solace and clarity. It left an indelible imprint on her soul, one that she continues to carry with her to this day.

She went to the barn where she kept the new horse she had rescued from Islip, New York. The big red horse had been knee-deep in muck in a small paddock, wet and exhausted from simply trying to move around. After a strenuous effort, they finally got him back to Maine and to a barn that a friend of my mom's had kindly offered for his care. The horse had a limp in his front left shoulder, and they soon discovered an abscess that had ruptured the moment the farrier touched it. He required daily care, including having his hoof soaked twice a day to aid in his recovery.

She walked into the big open barn and made her way to a quiet corner where her big red horse was resting. With her back turned to the other horses, she gently laid her hands on the shoulder of her newly rescued companion. In that moment, she felt an overwhelming sense of peace wash over her—a silence that was not empty but filled with a profound and indescribable comfort.

As she turned around, she was met with a sight that took her breath away. Behind her, all five of the other horses stood silently, their heads lowered and their eyes closed. They seemed to be enveloped in an almost sacred stillness, their soft breaths filling the space like a gentle rhythm. It was as if they were channeling a quiet, healing energy, surrounding her in a circle of unspoken understanding and care. It was a moment that touched her soul, one she would carry with her forever. But wait, what truly astonished her the most was that the big black horse named "Fella" was there as well. Fella, majestic and commanding, ruled the farm with an undeniable presence. He had a way of letting everyone know who was in charge—stomping his hooves, pinning his ears back, and declaring with his demeanor, "This is my space." My mom always respected his boundaries, honoring the unspoken request he made for his domain to remain undisturbed.

Yet, in that extraordinary moment, there he was, standing behind her, so close that she could almost feel the warmth of his breath on her shoulder. My mom had been so deeply immersed in her connection and healing with the newly rescued friend that she hadn't noticed Fella's approach—or, for that matter, the quiet arrival of the other horses that now surrounded her. They seemed to silently gather to offer their healing energy to both the big red and my mom.

As her new rescued friend, a chestnut gelding named H.B. (Halo Bars), stood there comforting my mom, the other horses came in to join him. Fella stood behind her quietly, then nudged her arm as if to say, "I see you." Her racing thoughts began to slow, and she felt an incredible sense of calm. She didn't need words to reassure her; their presence was enough. In those moments, she understood the innate gift horses offer—a nonjudgmental, grounding connection that allows the soul to rest. From that day forward, her relationship with Fella was different, and he would always come up to greet her to gently say his hellos, the master of the herd in his majestic frame and glimmering black coat. What an amazing gift she received that day.

I believe the horses were thanking her for rescuing H.B. and for taking care of him as he healed from the painful abscess in his hoof. The healing touch that my mom gave H.B. was felt amongst all the horses, and in return, they healed her right back. It was as though they shared a collective gratitude, a quiet acknowledgement that rippled through the barn each time she stepped into their world.

This moment became a cornerstone for her—a reminder of the profound exchange that exists between humans and animals, particularly horses. They aren't just companions; they are mirrors of our emotions, teachers of patience, and guides through the unbalanced paths of life. As she continued to care for H.B., she discovered not only his resilience but also her own. The barn became a sanctuary, a place where she could reconnect with herself through the unspoken wisdom of these magnificent creatures.

And so, with every soft whinny, every gentle nudge, and every moment of shared stillness, she found herself redefined—not just as a caretaker of H.B., but as part of a bigger, unspoken unity, one that she experiences here now where I live too. The horses, with their instinctive understanding, carried her burdens as if to say, "We've got you." And now I too share this message to her, "I've got you mom." And in turn, she carried forward this same message, sharing their burdens and creating a bond that was as healing as it was transformative. This message resonates deeply with me every time my mom comes to visit—or for that matter, when anyone comes to visit—but especially her. She is my rescuer, and I rescue her right back.

This is a picture of H.B. with my mom's mother riding him. His gentle soul taking great care of her as she is riding on his back. You can see him feeling her gentle touch of gratitude as they experienced this moment together. Another human being rescued and a bond that lasts a lifetime.

Here is some "Science" Behind Equine Therapy that I have learned:

"Equine therapy, also known as equine-assisted therapy, is supported by an increasing body of scientific evidence. Studies have shown that interactions with horses can lower stress levels, reduce symptoms of depression and anxiety, and improve overall emotional regulation. For example, a 2015 study published in the "Journal of Creativity in Mental Health" found that individuals who participated in equine-assisted activities experienced significant improvements in self-esteem, confidence, and coping strategies.

One of the mechanisms behind these benefits is the way horses mirror human emotions. You see, horses are highly sensitive to body language, tone, and energy. When a person is tense or unsettled, a horse may reflect that unease, prompting the individual to become more self-aware and adjust their behavior. This feedback loop fosters emotional growth and helps individuals develop healthier ways of managing their feelings.

Furthermore, being around horses engages the "parasympathetic nervous system," often referred to as the "rest and digest" system. The act of grooming a horse, feeling the warmth of its body, or simply watching it graze can trigger a relaxation response, lowering cortisol levels and promoting a sense of peace."

My mom and I do this type of therapy a lot as she takes me out to graze. I will feel her hand lay gently on my withers as she stands beside me absorbing my love and friendship as a deep bond entwined within our relationship.

These are all the types of experiences I see here at RiverView Farm. People connecting through their companions and friend, their horse, who rescues them right back as they journey this life together. And when I think of the Nakota people and their horses, the "Nokota horse," I see that same spirit—unbroken, resilient, and deeply intertwined with the land, their connections to the animals and how they honored each other. Their story reminds me of my own story and why I live my dream of being a Nokota.

It is said that the resilience of the Nakota people mirrored that of their horses, whose diversity—ranging from the agility of the Turkoman, to the endurance of the Fell Pony, to the strength of the Belgian Draft—embodied the ability to endure and thrive in the face of adversity. These horses, united under the care of the Nakota became a symbol of their enduring spirit and adaptation.

These traits and bloodlines run through my veins, tethering me to the boundless freedom of the Nokota spirit. In my dreams, I gallop untamed across the vast plains of the Dakotas.

At night, as I rest upon my shavings, my spirit roams those lands, hearing the echo of my ancestors' hoofbeats resonating across the open prairies. Those hoofbeats carry the enduring legacy of resilience and freedom.

The story of how the Turkoman horse, Fell Pony, and Belgian Draft became woven into this heritage serves as a powerful testament to the interconnectedness of cultures and histories. It reminds us that through migration, adaptation, and shared experiences, even the most distant heritages can converge, enriching the lives they touch and leaving a lasting imprint on the world.

As I dream of horses roaming the hills of the Dakotas, I see my ancestors so clearly. The thundering herd that marks the legacy of the Nokota horse in its true spirit, emerging from the fog and echoing their survival, inherent to the Nokota breed.

Here, my ancestors lived as free spirits, and if you visit these lands and close your eyes, you can still hear the thunderous hoofbeats as we live on in the hearts and minds of those who honor us.

Moments of Reflection from My Mom

Reflecting on the memories evoked by this book, one finds a deep sense of tradition rooted in genuine care for animals, and recognizes that, in truth, they also care for us.

As I look back on the stories in this book, I'm reminded of the joy and enduring spirit that comes with having a horse. The connection remains with you throughout your life. When I recall my parents—especially my mother—I'm struck by how she cherished horses from childhood into her later years. Even as an adult, she still had the courage to climb atop a horse and pursue those dreams that delighted her as a child.

Here is a photo of my mom thrilled to receive a pony when she moved to Standish, Maine. Notice how her smile radiates just like a child's and then compare it to the joyful expression she wore as a woman in her later years—each smile beams with happiness!

I remember how she used to fill her pockets before taking her daily walk around the village square—one pocket held dog treats, while the other was filled with carrots for the ponies on the corner. The moment the ponies spotted her, they would whinny with excitement, knowing her gentle touch and a tasty carrot were waiting for them.

Later, my dad joined her for walks around the Square, where years of building relationships led the animals to greet them. These strolls became cherished routines, filled with familiar faces—both human and animal alike. Over time, the gentle interactions cre-

ated a sense of community and comfort, making each walk a meaningful and memorable experience for both my dad and mom.

I have a special story to share with you. One day, as I walked past a picture hanging on my bedroom wall it stopped me in my tracks. It's a picture of my dad as a teenager riding his horse, and I was struck by how much that horse looks like my Maverick.

Seeing the resemblance made me pause and feel grateful for this photo—a reminder of my father's bond with his horse and the presence the horse's spirit still seems to have.

There are stories about when my father was in high school; sometimes he would bring his horse with him to school. In one story, I heard that he and a friend—both on horseback—were running late to school. They rode their horses up the steps and right into the schoolhouse! The trust between my father and his horse must have been extraordinary for the horse to follow him up those stairs and into the building just so my father could say, "I'm not late!"

These gifts hold special meaning for me; they symbolize treasured memories and the deep connections inherited from my ancestors. Maverick, too, longed to join the Nokota horses and found that his heritage was shaped by age-old stories, reflected in breeds like the Fell Pony, Turkoman, and Belgian Draft.

As I ponder these memories, I realize that a love for horses is woven throughout my family's history—connecting each generation with quiet understanding and tender affection. The horses we've known have served as companions and silent witnesses to our joys and struggles, helping carry our stories forward one gentle nicker and steady step at a time. Their presence continues to fill me with gratitude and wonder, showing that some bonds endure quietly, echoing through both spirit and memory.

Whether it was a dog or a pony, my parents always said their hellos to their friends waiting along their walks around the village square in Andover, Maine—each one eagerly watching for them to appear around the corner late in the day to get their treat. Just as Maverick waits for a white car to arrive on Sunday mornings, ears perked, racing to the fence for a hug and, of course, the carrots tucked away in mama's pockets.

"Celebrating RiverView Farm"

In the heart of Maine, RiverView Farm stands as a sanctuary for horses in need—offering them the opportunity to heal, thrive, and rediscover their own strength. Their dedication to natural horsemanship and personalized care has transformed the lives of countless horses, including Maverick, whose story is woven deeply with their generosity.

Through this book, "Maverick: I Dream of Being a Nokota," we extend gratitude to RiverView Farm by donating 40% of the profits to support their mission.

Just as Maverick carries the legacy of his ancestors with pride and resilience, RiverView Farm carries forward the spirit of kindness and connection, ensuring that every rescued horse has a chance to dream again.

NOKOTA
GRACE

NOKOTA G.R.A.C.E.

Graceful Partnership, **R**espect for Tradition, **A**ffirming
Wisdom, **C**elebrating Unity, **E**mpowering Healing

Nokota Grace is a sacred natural horsemanship program inspired by the spirit of Maverick and the ancestral heartbeat of RiverView Farm. Rooted in reverence, intuition, and gentle connection, it honors the Nokota lineage through soulful training practices. This program welcomes both horse and human into a shared journey of trust, healing, and reverence—guided by Maverick's enduring legacy and the living prayer of the land at RiverView Farm.

Let this be the way:

Of lightness in touch,
Of listening in silence,
Of grace in every stride.

Aho. Amen. Let it be so.

History tells us that the Nakota people developed a profound bond with their horses, rooted in mutual respect and spiritual connection. Their practices included gentle handling, intuitive communication, and honoring the horse as a sacred partner rather than simply an animal to be trained. Horses were integrated into daily life and ceremonies, reflecting the belief that they carried the prayers and hopes  of the people. This relationship was built on trust, patience, and a deep understanding of the horse's natural instincts, creating a partnership that went beyond utility to embrace healing and shared purpose.

We at **Nokota Grace** wish to honor this tradition through this program as we continue the sacred relationship, inviting participants to experience a tradition that heals the soul and feeds the earth with its enduring bond.

*"**Nokota Grace at RiverView Farm**" is a sanctuary devoted to healing, where the land and the spirit of the horse offer comfort and renewal. The horse-human connection is mindfully cultivated, honoring natural instincts and forming a partnership that embraces profound healing and purpose.*

Each moment of Nokota Grace celebrates the Nokota legacy, weaving together healing, harmony, and belonging for all who enter.

Founding Blessing: Nokota Grace at RiverView Farm

Today, I enter the pasture not to lead, but to listen. I lay down the halter of control and lift the reins of grace. Here, in the hush between hoofbeats, I hear the ancestors breathe. Feathers float in the wind, and Maverick stands as witness—free, whole, and wise.

RiverView flows beneath us, the land remembering every step,
The Nokota spirit rides beside me, whispering: "Be gentle. Be true."
I offer my heart, not my command. I offer my breath, not my bridle.
And in this sacred space, horse and human meet—
not in mastery, but in communion.

Let this be the way:

Of lightness in touch,
Of listening in silence,
Of grace in every stride.

Aho. Amen. Let it be so.

As Maverick's spirit awakens and ancient Nakota traditions are renewed, Nokota Grace stands as a beacon of unity and empowering healing for all.

We invite you to join our journey at RiverView Farm, 58 Edgecomb Rd., Lisbon Falls—where horse and human meet in harmony and hope.

NOKOTA GRACE
AT RIVERVIEW

Author's Note

As my journey continues in learning the gift of becoming an equine practitioner of healing, I am guided by the spirit of the horse—each one a vessel of wisdom, presence, and grace. Whether Nokota or otherwise, their essence speaks in silence, in movement, in the spaces between. The Nokota horse spirit, in particular, carries a legacy of resilience and intuitive knowing that echoes through every breath of this sanctuary. In their company, I am invited to remember what healing truly means: not to fix, but to feel; not to lead, but to listen.

These beings see what we can-
not see—they sense the tremble
beneath our words, the ache behind our silence, and respond with
a grace that transcends language.
This path is not linear—it is sacred, spiraling through land, lineage, and love. It is a devotion to the
unseen, and a partnership with the
soul of the horse.

This sacred work echoes the prophecy of Edgar Cayce, who foresaw
a time when horses would be honored not for labor or transportation, but for their spiritual and healing gifts. He spoke of horses as
mirrors—beings who reflect our inner royalty and help us remember
our divine heritage. In their presence, we learn love, trust, and reverence—not as concepts, but as embodied truths. Cayce envisioned
horses as healers of humanity's soul wounds, and here at Nokota Grace,
that vision breathes.

And when a moment of grace completes its arc—when healing is
witnessed, or a truth is finally spoken—I place a feather in Maverick's
image, honoring the spirit who first showed me the way. Nokota Grace
is not a method—it is a living ceremony, a call to remember, and an in-
vitation to walk the path of heart-led partnership and sacred exchange.

So, As you close this book, may the spirit of the Nokota walk beside
you—in silence, in breath, in grace.

A gift from Maverick who dreams of being a Nokota.

References

- Cowgirl Magazine article by Deborah Donahue

- https://en.wikipedia.org/wiki/Nokota_horse

- https://www.nokotahorse.org/

- https://www.nokotahorse.org/nokotareg-preservation-breed
  ers.html

- https://www.nokotahorse.org/nokotareg-history.html

- https://www.facebook.com/RiverViewHorseFarm/

- https://www.facebook.com/p/RiverView-Horse-Supply-Inc-6
  1572588331747/

www.ingramcontent.com/pod-product-compliance
Lightning Source LLC
Chambersburg PA
CBHW061716120626
46550CB00003B/1240